CELEBRATING HONEY·BEES

story by

Aaron William Perry

art by

Yvonne Kozlina

First Printing March 2019

Printed in the United States of America

Celebrating Honeybees

ISBN: 978-0-9986294-5-2 (pbk)

ISBN: 978-0-9986294-6-9 (ebk)

Library of Congress Control Number: 2019902312

Earth Water Press, Denver Colorado

www.earthwaterpress.com

To book this author for a speaking engagement or workshop, contact engage@yonearth.org

CELEBRATING HONEYBEES

Story by
AARON WILLIAM PERRY

Art by
YVONNE KOZLINA

Hi Friends!

My name is Sophia, and I'm a honey bee. I love flowers, sunshine and rainbows. I'm so excited to join you on this adventure Celebrating Honey Bees! Look for me in each picture: I'll be your friend and guide through the whole book!

We may encounter some new terms and concepts. Not to worry! The Y on Earth Community team has provided us resources at the back of the book, including a key word list for the bold, italicized words in the story, to help answer questions and share some special knowledge and inspiration with you!

Are you ready for an adventure together?

Buzzing with Love,

This morning during breakfast, Sister suggests to Brother, "Let's go visit the Old Man and the Old Lady today!"

Brother gets a huge smile on his face, saying, "Yes, that sounds wonderful!"

They ask Mother and Father if they could make the visit. Almost immediately after hearing Mother respond, "Yes, that sounds like a lovely idea," Sister and Brother hurry out the door, running and laughing down the path.

The Old Man and the Old Lady live in a cozy cottage in the woods, nestled along Sweet Water Creek. The walk to their cottage is full of surprises and delights: birds singing cheerfully overhead, deer grazing peacefully in the sunny glades, and chipmunks scurrying here and there gathering seeds and acorns.

About half-way to the cottage, Sister and Brother see a patch of emerald green moss carpeting the base of a giant oak tree. Sister suggests to Brother, "Let's sit on that moss patch, close our eyes, and listen quietly to the forest sounds!" She loves to listen to the trees, the wind, and the birds. And she especially loves the gentle, happy, buzzing sounds of the insects doing all of their busy life-work in the woods!

Brother happily sits down on the moss and closes his eyes. Then Sister does the same. They sit and listen to this living orchestra for many minutes.

Suddenly, Brother puts his hand on Sister's and whispers, "Do you hear that loud buzzing?"

"Yeah," whispers Sister in response, squeezing Brother's hand with excitement, "What do you think it is?"

"I don't know," replies Brother in a hushed voice. "Let's go find out!" He says, as they both open their eyes slowly to the bright scene surrounding them.

Their eyes adjust to the surrounding beauty. The landscape glimmers with an incredible brilliance. The whole scene is bathed in a green glow of the trees, awash with iridescent rainbow colors from the sunlight cascading through the leaves.

Sister points across the pond, "The buzzing is coming from over there!"

They approach slowly: it's a beehive! They're cautious and curious, and stand still watching the bees coming and going from the hive. They see a whole spray of bees departing the hive: flying off in slightly different directions toward the morning sun in the East. And, as Brother and Sister slowly walk closer to the hive, they notice several bees dancing in rhythmic, geometric patterns at the entrance of the hive.

"I wonder why they're dancing like that," inquired Sister with a giggle, "It looks like they're having so much fun!"

Brother and Sister are thrilled by their discovery and are bursting with excitement to tell their friends. "Let's go tell the Old Man and the Old Lady about the hive!" exclaims Brother.

"Yes, that sounds lovely!" agrees Sister.

They run and skip as quickly as they can to the Old Man's and Old Lady's cottage.

Arriving at the gate, Sister notices a sign hanging overhead:

"Welcome to Tom's & Goldberry's Humble Abode."

"That's funny," says Sister to Brother, smiling, "I didn't know they had names like that!"

"Yeah," agrees Brother, "I thought they are just called the Old Man and the Old Lady!"

The children go through the gate, and enter a flower garden that is bursting with color and activity: along with butterflies of all sizes and colors, hundreds of honey bees are going from flower to flower gathering **pollen** and **nectar** from the **blossoms**.

"Wow," whispered Brother, "That's so beautiful!"

"Yeah," agrees Sister, "It's like a painting!"

Sister pulls Brother gently by the hand, exclaiming, "Come on, let's go knock on the door!"

They approach a beautifully carved wooden door, set perfectly in sturdy arched masonry. Although in a simple cottage, the smooth stone arch over the door way reminds Sister of the *cathedral* they recently saw in the Old City.

Brother walks up onto the stoop, standing tall, and knocks three bold raps on the thick wooden door.

"Coming!" they hear a woman's *harmonious* voice sing out from within: that must be the Old Lady!

The door glides open and their friend the Old Lady is standing in the *foyer*: "Oh hello dear children!" she welcomes them warmly, "Come in, come in! . . . You're just in time! I'm about to pull a fresh loaf of my home-made *sourdough bread* out of the oven!"

The comforting aroma of baking bread envelops Brother and Sister as they walk into the cozy cottage: it smells nutty, earthy and sweet all at once! They walk down the hall, which is decorated with the Old Man's paintings and the Old Lady's pottery, and into the sun-lit kitchen where the Old Man is sitting at the table sipping tea. "Oh, hello my friends!" bellows the Old Man in his jolly way, "Welcome, welcome!"

"Hello, hello!" sings Sister in response.

"Good day Sir!" greets Brother, with a playful air of formality, "How are you this fine day?"

"Oh dear friends, I'm splendid!" bellows the Old Man, "I couldn't be better! I just love it when Goldberry makes fresh bread, and I just gathered honey from our friends the honey bees. You're just in time, we can enjoy all of this together!"

Humming and smiling, the Old Lady pulls the steaming bread from the oven. The Old Man gathers the pot of honey, some herbal tea, and several hand-made ceramic mugs from the cupboard.

They all sit at the wooden table and enjoy the delicious bread, drizzled with sweet, fragrant honey. The smells of the bread and honey together remind Brother and Sister of some far off memory: maybe from a dream? Or an ancient cozy memory of their ancestors, somehow lodged in the libraries of their own **DNA**?

"This bread is made from my special sourdough starter: which is a community of millions of tiny friends, tiny organisms, who help make the bread super delicious and super nutritious!"

Sister and Brother take giant bites of their bread and honey, and marvel at the idea that those invisible little critters could make the bread so good. "And the honey bees make such wonderful honey!" exclaims Sister, licking the sweetness on her lips.

"They do indeed!" Smiles the Old Lady, "And they pollinate so many of our foods as well. They fertilizing the leafy trees, the bushes, and the vines that produce our fruits and vegetables: from A to Z, from apples to zucchini, and so many in between!"

"And," adds the Old Man, "we help to take care of them by planting special forage plants, by keeping poisonous pesticides far away, and by tending their hives with care. We are in a beautiful, *cooperative* partnership with the honey bees!"

As they are finishing up their marvelous snack, the Old Lady says, "Let's go say hi to the hive and get some honey for your mother and father!"

"A splendid idea!" agrees the Old Man, "Let's go out in the garden and visit the hive!"

Out in the garden, Brother exclaims, "Wow, that's amazing!"

"Come closer, look in here," invites the Old Man. "I'll open the viewing window so that we can see what's going on inside the hive."

Brother and Sister had never been so close to a beehive before: they kept their distance from the one they saw earlier in the woods. "Will we get stung?" asks Sister, in a concerned tone.

"No, no, that's not likely," assures the Old Man, "We just have to approach the hive very calmly and with loving kindness in our hearts."

As they walk toward the hive, the Old Man begins humming a beautiful low tone, and the Old Lady sings a sweet melody. The bees are busy flying in and out of the entrance. And Brother sees they are dancing that same rhythmic dance they saw at the wild hive in the woods.

"What are they doing?" asks Brother.

"They're dancing to communicate with each other!" explains the Old Lady. "By dancing in certain *geometric* shapes and *rhythmic* patterns, they are telling each other where they've been and what they've seen and tasted: perhaps where there's an abundant flow of nectar, or some cool, clean water. Honey bees communicate with special ritual dance ceremonies every day!"

Sister leans in and sees a dozen *honeycomb* structures lined up in neat rows. "That's amazing," she exclaims, "Look at how many bees there are inside! And, my goodness, how do they build such amazing forms?"

Those honeycombs are all built by honey bees, using wax that they *alchemically* produce within their own bodies from honey. As the bees are building the honeycomb, they *vibrate* their bodies to help form the structure inside the hive: you could say they actually sing the forms into being! The *hexagonal* shape is one of the strongest, lightest structures found in nature. You see, honey bees are master builders, and have inspired many great human carpenters and masons to build beautiful, strong, elegant structures as well! In fact the bees and their honeycombs and hives are one of the special symbols that stone masons and wood carvers use to identify their craft guilds all over the world.

Brother and Sister are speechless, deep in *mystified* thought as they gaze at the interior of the hive, recalling images of the great cathedrals and castles they've seen in the Old City.

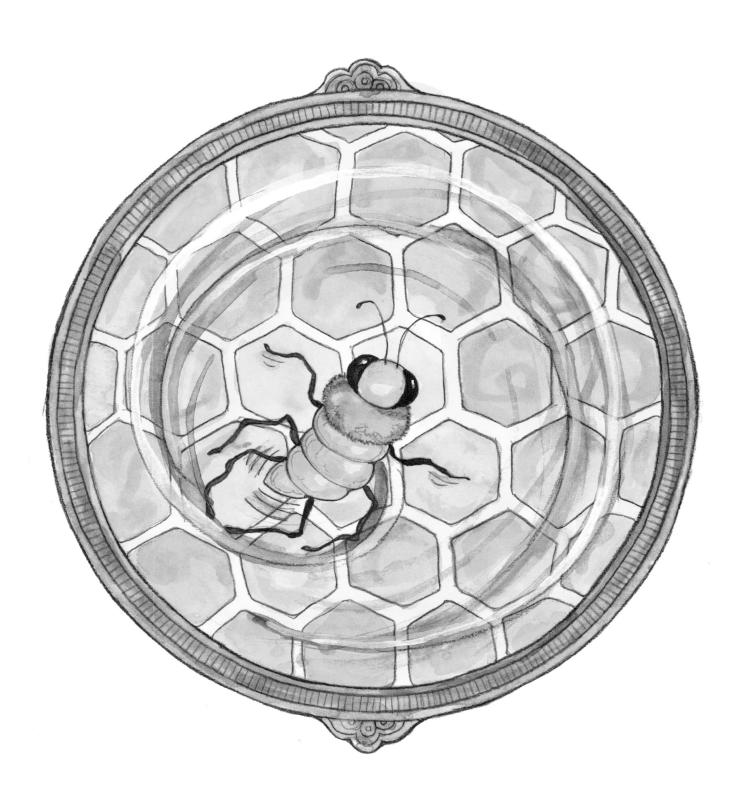

"The hive is their cathedral, their lodge," continues the Old Man. "And they take great care of it and of each other. Like a single **super-organism**, they work in peace and harmony to ensure the safety and **prosperity** of the hive and of each other!"

"And, they help connect entire **ecosystems** together, visiting all of the flowers and harvesting the liquid sunshine of the flowers' nectar and golden pollen to make beeswax, honey, and a special material called **propolis**!"

"But honey bees aren't the only type of bee," explains the Old Lady. "There's even a special type of solitary bee called a Mason Bee. Not all of the bee species are social bees, some live their lives alone, but are also very important **pollinators** that visit and pollinate thousands of different plant species throughout the landscape. Mason Bees can often be green or bright blue in color," she says as she points toward a pink flower, "There's one now!"

"That pink flower gives off special vibrating colors, **frequencies**, and scents that attract all kinds of bees and other pollinators to its pollen and nectar: just as all the other flowers are doing all around us," chimes in the Old Man, "It's like the whole landscape is alive with communication and interaction: and the bees are key connectors and messengers!"

"Mason Bees are solo creatures," continues the Old Lady," but honey bees represent the sweet virtues of communities working and cooperating together to achieve common goals, and to take care of each other."

As the Old Lady explains the miracle of the super organism, Brother counts 33 honey bees taking off from the entrance of the hive, and flying off toward the east. "How do they know where to go?" Brother asks, watching them disappear into the distant trees.

"They navigate using the position of the sun!" replies the Old Lady, as she spreads her arms and starts dancing around the garden, imitating a bee in flight. "And, as they flap and buzz their *translucent* wings, they help scatter the radiant sunlight in its full rainbow of colors, using their wings as *prisms* to disperse the life-giving light to the flowers and bushes and trees. They're painting with sunshine throughout the gardens and forests: spreading *sacred* sunlight *fertilizer* that nourishes our world!

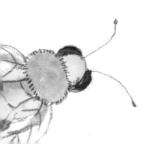

"That's amazing!" exclaims Brother, joining the Old Lady in her honey bee dance, "What fun!"

"What joy!" shouts Sister with a smile.

"They fly through the forest and gardens, gathering nectar from the blossoms, which they convert into honey like a lodge full of happy alchemists!" explained the Old Lady. "From their precise geometric building, to their amazing dancing and navigation, to their magical ability to transform nectar to honey and honey into beeswax, the honey bees are one of the most fascinating creatures on Earth!"

"Do you see that one?" asks the Old Man, pointing at a slightly larger honey bee landing on the entrance of the hive. "That's a drone: one of the communicator bees that travels and visits many hives to share information and to network with the other honey bee communities in the area. The drones are like the *bards* and *emissaries* of *yore*: they go from colony to colony gathering and sharing information!"

"This allows the hives to coordinate and cooperate as super-organisms throughout the landscape: they are *keystone stewards* of the forests, the fields, and our orchards and gardens!" explains the Old Lady. "And," she continues, "They aren't the only pollinators in the ecosystem. Butterflies, birds, bats, lizards and even monkeys also pollinate the flowering and fruiting plants throughout Earth's ecosystems!"

"All of these pollinators are doing very important work in the ecosystems we depend on, and they really need our help!" the Old Lady explains. "We have to help them out by planting special *forage* plants to provide them abundant food and by making sure none of our neighbors are using poisonous pesticides that can kill the honey bees and other pollinators. It's so important that we do this work, and that we encourage our friends and neighbors to do the same: helping to create bee-safe neighborhoods throughout the land!"

"I will definitely help!" exclaims Sister, "I will plant the special plants in our yard, and I will tell my friends and neighbors to take care of the honey bees!"

"I will too!" chimes in Brother, "I will ask my teacher if we can have a class discussion about taking care of the honey bees so that all of my schoolmates learn this too!"

"Wonderful!" the Old Lady responds, as she dances around the hive, "That's just wonderful!"

"If you can each help at least ten others to become *bee guardians*, and they do the same," explains the Old Man, "Very soon the honey bees and other pollinators will be so well cared for: they will be safe and happy, and will help heal and restore ecosystems all over the world!"

"Yes, we will!" shout Brother and Sister together, "We will become bee guardians like you!"

The End

About the Y on Earth Community

The Y on Earth Community is a growing movement of students, parents, teachers, entrepreneurs, executives, and organizational leaders helping to mobilize stewardship and sustainability throughout our culture.

We provide powerful, accessible tools and hope-filled inspiration to enhance day-to-day health and well being while deeply aligning with global strategies for regeneration, stewardship, and sustainability. Our simple and empowering tools for "Thriving"— in the domains of soil, gardens, food, nature, and stewardship—are fun for children of all ages!

You will find additional children's books, videos, resources, and activity guides at yonearth.org. Be sure to check out our Stewardship & Sustainability Podcast series on the website as well!

SPONSORS

The following companies and organizations are collaborating supporters of the Y on Earth Community: helping to cultivate a culture of stewardship and sustainability. Use the code: **YONEARTH** to get special deals and discounts at their websites!

Calls To Action

You can help the honey bees, pollinators and other insects in your yard, neighborhood, school, and community. Here are eight important ways you can help out!

1. Stop poisoning yards and landscapes with harmful pesticides, including all insecticides, herbicides, fungicides and synthetic fertilizers as well.

2. Plant pollinator-friendly wild-flower gardens everywhere you can.

3. Leave part of your garden, yard or neighborhood park in a wild state.

4. Buy organic and biodynamic food, beverage and clothing products: this helps protect other places, pollinators, and people all around the world!

5. Join or create a bee-safe neighborhood where you live.

6. Plant gardens and help keep bees at your school or your parents' workplace.

7. Share this information and these fun activities with your friends and neighbors.

8. Celebrate World Bee Day with our global community every May 20th!

The Xerces Society

The Xerces Society for Invertebrate Conservation is a leader in pollinator protection. You will find excellent resources on the www.xerces.org website, including:

- Pollinator Conservation
- Pollinator-Friendly Plant Lists
- Bee Information
- Monarch Conservation

THE XERCES SOCIETY
POLLINATOR CONSERVATION PROGRAM

Bee Safe Neighborhoods

The Bee-Safe Neighborhood program, created by the Living Systems Institute, is a fun, neighbor-friendly framework for creating pollinator-safe habitat throughout neighborhoods and communities. You can start a Bee Safe Neighborhood in your community, or join one that's already established and help spread the message!

www.livingsystemsinst.org/project/bee-safe-neighborhoods-0

www.livingsystemsinst.org

Our Pollinated Foods

Insect pollinators—especially honey bees—pollinate over $4 billion of fruits and vegetables every year—food that would not otherwise be available! This list of examples, from A to Z, probably includes some of your favorites!

Alfalfa	Cashews	Grapefruit	Peppermint
Almonds	Cherries	Kiwifruit	Pumpkins
Anise	Chocolate	Macadamia Nuts	Raspberries
Apples	Coconut	Mangoes	Sesame
Apricots	Coffee	Melons	Strawberries
Avocados	Coriander	Nutmeg	Tea
Bananas	Cranberries	Papayas	Tomatoes
Blueberries	Figs	Peaches	Vanilla
Cardamom	Grapes	Pears	Zucchini

Protect their lives. Preserve ours.

KEY WORD LIST

Abode: a place of residence, house, home.

Alchemical: involving a seemingly magical process of transformation, creation, or combination.

Bard: a poet, traditionally one who travels between villages and recites epic poetry in the oral tradition.

Bee Guardians: individuals and communities who take care of honey bees with natural, chemical-free methods and a commitment to stewardship, as established by Master Bee-Keeper, Corwin Bell.

Blossom: a flower or mass of flowers, especially on trees and bushes.

Cathedral: the principal house of worship in many regions, usually usually built of stone masonry, and typically of medieval origin, especially in Europe and the Mediterranean regions.

Cooperative: involving mutual assistance in working toward a common goal, including farming, business, and community organizations structured for the benefit of its members.

DNA: deoxyribonucleic acid, a self-replicating material which is present in nearly all living organisms as the main constituent of chromosomes. It is the carrier of genetic information, and is increasingly being studied as the potential carrier of "epigenetic" or trans-generational memory and information.

Ecosystem: a biological community of interacting organisms and their physical environment, also (in general use) a complex network or interconnected system.

Emissary: a person sent on a special mission, usually as a diplomatic representative.

Fertilizer: a substance added to soil or land to increase its fertility, or ability to grow and thrive.

Forage: food or fodder.

Foyer: an entrance hall or other open area in a building, especially in homes, theaters, or hotels.

Frequency: the rate at which a vibration occurs that constitutes a wave, either in a material (as in sound waves), or in an electromagnetic field (as in radio waves and light), usually measured per second.

Geometric: relating to geometry (from Greek: Earth-measure), decorated or adorned with regular lines and shapes.

Harmonious: tuneful; not discordant, forming a pleasing or consistent whole, or free from disagreement or dissent.

Hexagonal: pertaining to a six-sided shape of equal side-lengths and angles, or pertaining to a crystal system in which three coplanar axes of equal length are separated by 60° and a fourth axis of a different length is at right angles to these.

Honeycomb: structure of hexagonal cells of wax, made by bees to store honey and eggs.

Humble: having or showing a modest estimate of one's own importance, of or relating to the soil (humus), deliberately working in service to something greater than oneself.

Keystone: a central stone at the summit of an arch, locking the whole together, or the central principle or part of a policy, system, etc., on which all else depends.

Mystify: make obscure or mysterious, including in a spiritual or reverential sense.

Nectar: a sugary fluid secreted by plants, especially within flowers to encourage pollination by insects and other animals. It is collected by bees to make into honey. In Greek and Roman mythology, the drink of the gods.

Pollen: a fine powdery substance, typically yellow, consisting of microscopic grains discharged from the male part of a flower or from a male pine-cone, that is essential to plant reproduction, often transferred with the help of pollinating insects.

Pollinators: an animal or insect that moves pollen from the male anther of a flower to the female stigma of a flower.

Prism: a glass or other transparent object with refracting surfaces at an acute angle with each other and that separates full-spectrum "white" light, or sunlight, into a spectrum of colors.

Propolis: a red or brown resinous substance collected by honeybees from tree buds, used by them to fill crevices and to seal and varnish honeycombs.

Prosperity: a state of good fortune, plenty, abundance and well-being.

Rhythmic: having a strong, regular, repeated pattern of movement or sound.

Sacred: connected with a higher purpose, God, and/or the Divine, and so deserving veneration.

Sourdough bread: leavened bread made from a living "culture" of microorganisms that proliferate in the dough fermentation process, typically left over from a previous batch, and giving the bread its distinctive flavor and additional nutrient density.

Stewards: people who look after, take care of, or otherwise tend and keep something, someone, or an ecosystem of living organisms.

Super-organism: a group or community of synergistically interacting organisms of the same species, in which the individuals have specialized roles, and a body of individuals which act in concert to produce phenomena governed by the collective.

Translucent: a substance allowing light, but not detailed shapes, to pass through; semitransparent.

Vibrate: move or cause to move continuously and rapidly to and fro, quiver, resonate (as with sound).

Yore: of long ago or former times, often used in nostalgic recollection.

ACKNOWLEDGEMENTS

It takes a whole village to create and publish these children's books! Yvonne and Aaron wish to say a very special thank-you to the following people who generously shared their knowledge and expertise, who supported the project, and who helped make *Celebrating Honey Bees* come alive.

Al & Christina Stemp

Anna Potter

Artem Nikulkov

Beverly Amico

Brad Lidge

Bruce Bridges

Corwin Bell

Courtney Cosgriff

Jack Dawson

Katie Garces

Kevin Townley

Maggie McLaughlin

Marcia Perry

Nita Davanzo

Sina Simantob

Travis Robinson

Thank You!

About the Author

Author and founder of the Y on Earth Community, Aaron William Perry is an entrepreneur, writer, speaker, consultant, and father. The author of *Y on Earth: Get Smarter, Feel Better, Heal the Planet*, Aaron works with the Y on Earth Community and Impact Ambassadors to spread the THRIVING and SUSTAINABILITY messages of hopeful and empowering information and inspiration to diverse communities throughout the world. He resides in Colorado where he loves to hike in the mountains, is continually in awe of the ever-changing weather, and entertained by the hilarious antics of his backyard, free-range (and free-thinking) chickens.

About the Illustrator

Yvonne Kozlina is a professional portrait artist and painter who originally hails from Pittsburgh, Pennsylvania and now makes Colorado her home. A mother and grandmother, She loves children and has taught art to diverse children of all ages. Yvonne's photo-realistic style is uncanny, as she taps in to the essence of the people she paints and draws. She is also an avid animal lover, gardener, and enjoys taking walks through the neighborhood when she isn't at her easel painting. See Yvonne's artwork and learn more about her custom portrait services at yvonnekozlina.com.

See you later!

Made in the USA
Lexington, KY
12 November 2019